This
Adu
The
requ

CONTINENTS
OF THE WORLD

ASIA

Rob Bowden

First published in 2005 by Hodder Wayland,
an imprint of Hodder Children's Books

© Hodder Wayland 2005

Commissioning editor: Victoria Brooker
Inside design: Jane Hawkins

Cover design: Hodder Wayland
Series concept and project management by
EASI-Educational Resourcing
(info@easi-er.co.uk) Statistical research: Anna Bowden

Population Distribution Map
© 2003 UT-Battelle, LLC. All rights reserved.
Data for population distribution maps reproduced under licence from
UT-Battelle, LLC. All rights reserved

Maps and graphs: Martin Darlison, Encompass Graphics

British Library Cataloguing in Publication Data

Bowden, Rob
 Asia. – (Continents of the world)
 1. Asia – Juvenile literature
 2. I.Title
 3. 980

ISBN 0 7502 4679 0

Printed and bound in China

Hodder Children's Books
A division of Hodder Headline Limited
338 Euston Road, London NW1 3BH

Picture acknowledgements
The author and publisher would like to thank the following for allowing their pictures to be reproduced in
this publication:
Chris Fairclough Worldwide 4, 9, 45 top: Christine Osborne Pictures 39: Corbis: 6 Yann Arthus-Bertrand;
7 Michael S. Yamashita; 8 Araldo de Luca; 11 Robert Essel NYC; 12 Bettmann; 13 Ahmad
Masood/Reuters; 14, 34 (top) Macduff Everton; 15 Kimimasa Mayama/Reuters; 16 Michael S. Yamashita;
17 David Turnley; 18 Wolfgang Kaehler; 20 Wolfgang Kaehler; 22 Bohemian Nomad Picturemakers; 23
Shepard Sherbell/Corbis Saba; 24 Howard Davies; 28 Alison Wright; 29 Beawiharta/Reuters; 30 Liu
Liqun; 33 (bottom) Kimimasa Mayama/Reuters; 35 Max Rossi/Reuters; 36 The Cover Story; 37 Peter
Blakely/Corbis Saba; 38 Colin Garratt; 42 Ed Kashi; 44 Jose Fuste Raga; 45 (bottom) Jagadeesh
Nv/Reuters; 48 East/Reuters; 49 Langevin Jacques/Corbis Sygma; 19, 50, 51, 58 Reuters; 53 Jeremy
Horner; main cover image and 54, 59 Keren Su; 55 D. Robert & Lorri Fran; 56 Theo Allofs: EASI-
Images/Tony Binns 1, 3, 10 (bottom), 25, 26, 40, 47 and 52; Rob Bowden cover inset and 34 (bottom) 20
(bottom), 27, 33 (top), 41, 43, 46, 57 ; Roy Maconachie 31; Miguel Hunt 32: Mary Evans Picture Library
10 (top).

Cover picture: Elaborate costumes and make up add to the drama of
kathakali dancing in Southern India

The skyline of Hong Kong is just one symbol of
Asia's emergence as a global economic centre
during the twentieth century.

CONTENTS

ASIA – THE LAND OF PEOPLE

Asia's fifty countries make up a vast continent of around 45,500,000 square kilometres (17,568,000 square miles), or 34 per cent of the world's total land area. It stretches from Europe in the west to Japan in the east and almost reaches Australia in the south-east. Asia also includes the predominantly Arabic nations of the Middle East and the majority of Russia, the world's largest country.

The most striking thing about Asia is its enormous population. In 2003, Asia accounted for almost two thirds of the world population – an incredible 4 billion people. China alone had a population of 1.3 billion with India not far behind with 1.1 billion. There are hundreds of distinct ethnic groups across Asia ranging from the Chukchi and Nenet who live in Russia's frozen Arctic, to the Karen and Hanunoo who inhabit the tropics of South-east Asia.

Asia's landscapes include the world's highest mountain range, the Himalayas, and several major deserts, including the Arabian and Gobi deserts. Many of the world's largest rivers, including the Yangtze, Ganges, Indus and Mekong, are also found in Asia. In the far east Asia becomes a continent of islands. Some are large, such as the main islands of Japan and Indonesia, but there are countless smaller islands with some 13,600 in Indonesia alone.

Economically, Asia is becoming one of the world's most powerful regions. Japan has by far the largest economy (second to the United States in world terms), but China is catching up fast. Since the early 1990s it

Shanghai, with an estimated 12.7 million people, is the largest city in China – the world's most populous country.

has been one of the world's fastest growing economies with an annual growth rate averaging nearly 10 per cent between 1991 and 2002. The oil-rich countries of the Middle East, such as Saudi Arabia and Kuwait, are also important economically and play a key role in global energy supplies. In stark contrast, Asia also has some of the world's poorest countries where life for many is a daily struggle against disease and malnutrition. These countries include Afghanistan, Bangladesh and Nepal.

Asia has the potential to become the world's most important continent in the twenty-first century both politically and economically. Optimism for its future is marred, however, by ongoing tensions and conflicts from Israel and Palestine in the west to North and South Korea in the east.

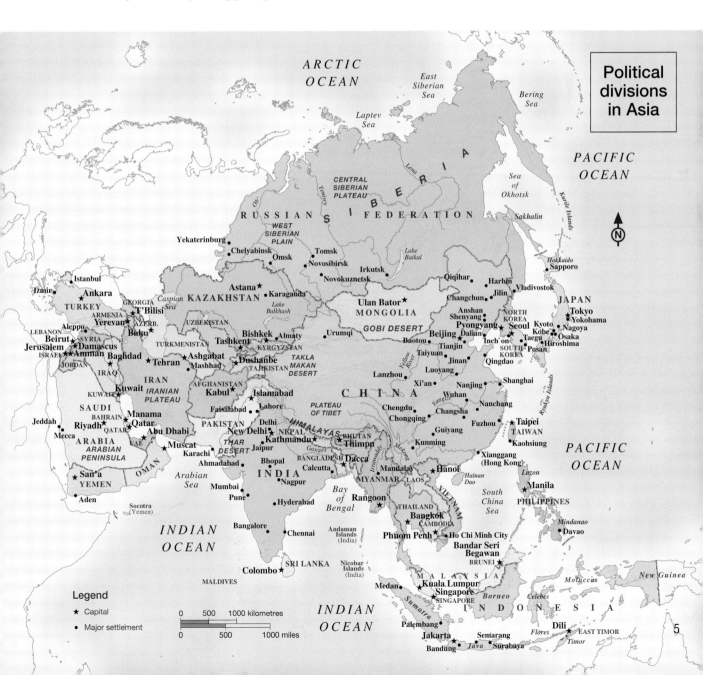

Political divisions in Asia

Legend

★ Capital

• Major settlement

0 500 1000 kilometres

0 500 1000 miles

1. THE HISTORY OF ASIA

MANY OF THE THINGS THAT WE TODAY TAKE FOR GRANTED EMERGED out of Asia's long and complex history. Asians are thought to have been the first to domesticate plants and animals in around 8000 BC. This development enabled people to engage in activities other than hunting and gathering for the first time, and as a result, some of the first known human settlements emerged in Jericho (Israeli-controlled West Bank) and Catal Huyuk (Turkey). Since these early days Asia has played a prominent role in world history from early civilizations and great empires through to major wars and groundbreaking achievements.

Archaeologists excavate the remains of early human settlement at Catal Huyuk in Turkey. The settlement is thought to date back to 7000 BC.

EARLY SETTLEMENT

The earliest evidence of human life in Asia is found in western China and the Indonesian island of Java. In both locations, remains of Homo erectus (ancestor of modern humans) have been found that date back 1.7 to 1.3 million years. Basic stone tools and evidence of the use of fire were discovered. Other remains dating back around 0.6 million years have been made in Vietnam, Thailand and Korea.

The first modern humans (*Homo sapiens sapiens*) arrived in western Asia from Africa around 100,000 years ago and, from there, spread eastwards reaching Japan around 50,000 years ago and northern Siberia around 30,000 years ago.

The ziggurat of Ur was the centrepiece of the ancient Sumerian city of Ur in modern day Iraq. The ziggurat was built as a temple to the moon god Nanna.

Asia also acted as the corridor for the expansion of modern humans into the Americas from across the Bering Strait around 15,000 years ago, and into Australia about 50,000 years ago.

FIRST CIVILIZATIONS

Around 3500 BC agriculture in the Tigris and Euphrates river valleys (an area known as Mesopotamia) had become so successful that wealthy individuals and families began to divert labour and resources into building impressive ceremonial temples. These became the focus for the world's first known civilization – the Sumerians – in what is today Iraq. Farming communities gathered around these temples and small villages turned into organised cities and centres of trade and craft. Lagosh, Uruk, Umma and Ur were among the most significant of these. The success of the Sumerians and later Mesopotamian cultures depended on their ability to redirect water from the Tigris and Euphrates rivers to their fields through a system of irrigation canals. This same factor was central to one of Asia's other early civilizations in the Indus river valley of Pakistan.

Agricultural towns first appeared in the Indus valley around 3500 BC, but it was not until 2500 BC that a major civilization emerged. Mohenjo-daro was one of the key cities of the Indus Valley Civilization. Archaeological finds show that besides farming it had well established trade links with Mesopotamia and Ancient Egypt. This advanced civilization collapsed around 2000 BC for reasons that are not fully known. A change in the course of the Indus river is the most likely explanation.

In China, the Shang civilization emerged around 1800 BC and remained a major power for about 700 years. The Shang dynasty does not appear to have developed extensive trade networks. Skilled craftsmanship, however, especially in bronze and lacquer work, did emerge as one of the Shang dynasty's main characteristics.

AGE OF EMPIRE

By around 1000 BC several of Asia's early civilizations developed into super-states with powerful armies. This marked an age of empire and warfare as successive Asian societies fought for control over large areas of the continent. The Assyrians were one of the first great empires and from their capital, in today's northern Iraq, they managed to unite and control much of western Asia for the first time. Subsequent empires followed, including the Babylonians and the Persians. One of the most famous, though short-lived, empires was that of Alexander the Great. An outstanding military general, he led the Greek army in the defeat of the Persians and gained control of large parts of western and central Asia between 334 and 323 BC .

This detail from a mosaic originally located in Pompeii shows Alexander the Great as a great warrior during the Battle of Issus in 333 BC. Alexander won the battle, defeating the Persian King Darius.

CHANGE AND DIVISION

The period from 300 BC to AD 1600 saw dramatic changes across Asia. In around 221 BC, China emerged as a unified state under Qin Shi Huangdi. The Mauryan Empire (325 BC-185 BC)

similarly unified much of India, a process continued several centuries later under the Hindu Gupta dynasty (AD 320-515) – a period of stability and great learning in India. Other important events during this period included the advent of Christianity, founded on the teachings of Jesus Christ who was crucified in Jerusalem in AD 33, and of Islam, founded on the teachings of the Prophet Muhammad who died in Mecca, Saudi Arabia in AD 632.

Up until the ninth century, as the most powerful state in east Asia, China had been extremely influential on its neighbouring territories in terms of language and culture. In the ninth century this influence began to decline and several new states began to emerge. In Cambodia, the Khmer empire developed (c.AD 802), and in Japan, the establishment of a new capital at Heian (Kyoto) saw the beginnings of a more distinctive Japanese culture, less aligned with China.

Between 1200 and 1600 a wave of new empires swept across Asia. Genghis Khan of Mongolia led the brutal forces of the Mongol Empire to conquer Central Asia and China, while the Turkish and Islamic Ottoman Empire reached its height under Sulayman the Magnificent (1520-66). The Mogul Empire also developed during this time (c.1504) from its base in Kabul, Afghanistan and had gained control over most of India by around 1700. Although Islamic, the Moguls were tolerant of India's Hindu population and a distinctive Indo-Muslim artistic culture emerged that is still evident in many of India's palaces and temples.

The Terracotta Army near Xian in China was made to protect the spirit of Qin Shi Huangdi (259-210 BC), the first emperor of China in his death. Containing some 8000 life-size warriors the army was discovered in 1974 by villagers digging a well.

FACT FILE

Buddhism was created as a religion following the teachings of Siddartha Gautama who lived in northern India between 560-482 BC.

Jakarta in Indonesia was a major shipping and trade port for the colonies of the Dutch East Indies. During Dutch control (1619-1949) it was known as Batavia.

COLONIAL ASIA

The period from 1600 to 1945 saw large parts of Asia come under the control of European maritime nations. The first contact with Europeans came through Portuguese spice traders, but other European nations - specifically the Spanish, Dutch, French and British - soon sought their own share of this lucrative trade. Representatives of these countries established coastal ports to supply and transport Asian produce back to Europe. Several of these ports are now among Asia's biggest cities, including Kolkata, Karachi, Singapore, Hong Kong, Jakarta and Shanghai. Over time, the European nations used their wealth and military superiority to impose colonial rule over large areas of the continent. During this period, the colonial powers extracted raw materials from their Asian colonies for export to Europe and then imported finished products back into the colonies. This practice undermined many local industries and consolidated national resources into the hands of a privileged few – a pattern that persists in many countries today.

Hong Kong's famous ferries sail the waters between Kowloon peninsula and Hong Kong Island. Hong Kong returned to Chinese administration in 1997 having been a British trading port since 1842.

FACT FILE

Between 1862 and 1943 the United States held a trading post called Hongkew in the Chinese city of Shanghai. The trading post was granted by the British following their victory over China in a war over trading rights in 1842.

CENTURY OF TURMOIL

The twentieth century in Asia was marked by conflict and revolution. The early part of the century saw China emerge from almost 2000 years of dynastic rule when Sun Zhongshan formed a united China in 1911. Unification was short-lived, however, and from 1912, power struggles and civil war led to a fragmented China controlled by numerous warlords. The first half of the twentieth century saw Japan emerge as a major Asian power and conquer much of eastern China as part of its empire. The Japanese also conquered Korea and Taiwan, but further expansionist ambitions brought the Japanese empire into conflict with the United States and Britain, which had both previously supported Japan. On 7 December 1941 the Japanese attacked a US naval base in Hawaii and pulled the US into World War II. The United States eventually signalled the beginning of the end of World War II when it dropped two atomic bombs on the Japanese cities of Hiroshima and Nagasaki in August 1945.

The A-Bomb Dome in Hiroshima, Japan was one of the few buildings left standing after the U.S. bombed the city in 1945. The shell of the building is now a permanent memorial to the tragedy and has become a symbol for peace.

World War II severely weakened Europe and as a result most Asian colonies were able to gain their independence in the years that followed. The Indian subcontinent gained independence from Britain in 1947 and was split by a process known as 'partition' to become three independent countries, Pakistan, India and Bangladesh (East Pakistan until 1971). In 1947 another British colony, Palestine, was divided by the United Nations into an Arab and Jewish state. Arabs rejected the plan, however, and fighting broke out that led to the creation of the Jewish state of Israel in May 1948. Further fighting between Arab countries and Israel has continued ever since with major wars over the control of lands in and around Israel, erupting in 1956, 1967 and 1973. Disputes over land have still to be settled and an almost continuous tension and violence remains between Israel and the Palestinians (the Arabic people who claim rights to the land).

COMMUNIST ASIA

After World War II the Union of Soviet Socialist Republics (USSR) emerged as a major superpower to rival the power of the United States. The two countries had very different beliefs. The USA believed in democracy and a free economic market, whereas the USSR had followed a communist path of development since the Russian revolution of 1917. Communism is a social and political ideology in which class systems are abolished and property and wealth are centrally owned and controlled by the community, for the community. In reality, Soviet communism led to the government's control of almost all aspects of life (where people lived, studied, worked).

Many nations around the world aligned themselves behind one of these beliefs in what came to be known as the 'Cold War'. China became a communist state in 1949 under Mao Zedong, and by the 1950s communist ideas were spreading into Southeast Asia. Keen to repel the advance of communism here the USA became heavily involved in the politics of the region. Nowhere was this more so than in Vietnam where the USA fought a long and costly war (1964-75) in a failed attempt to prevent communist North Vietnam from capturing non-communist southern Vietnam.

U.S. soldiers from a 3rd Brigade, 25th Division task force enter a Vietnamese village in May 1967, during operations as part of the Vietnam War.

The Cold War came to an end in 1991 following the collapse and break-up of the USSR. Many of Asia's newest states such as Kazakhstan, Georgia and Azerbaijan emerged as a result of this break up and all of the former Soviet states are now adopting and adjusting to the ideas of democratic governance and the free market. China and North Korea are the last remaining communist states in Asia.

A TURBULENT TURN

In 1990 a dispute over oil led to Iraq invading neighbouring Kuwait and declaring it a province of Iraq. The international community demanded Iraq's withdrawal, but when Iraq dictator Saddam Hussein refused, the US led an international coalition to successfully recapture Kuwait in the 1991 Gulf War. Saddam Hussein remained in power, however, and international sanctions failed to topple his Iraqi regime, which eventually fell following US-led military action in 2003 (see page 50). In 1996, an armed group called the Taliban took control (with support from Pakistan, Saudi Arabia and the USA) of Afghanistan after years of infighting between rival groups. Once in power, the Taliban introduced a strict and brutal Islamic regime that quickly attracted world criticism for its abuses of human rights. US-led forces invaded Afghanistan and removed the Taliban from power in late 2001. After a period of rebuilding, democratic elections were held in October 2004 to elect a new Afghan government. Events in Iraq and Afghanistan mark a turbulent turning of the century for Asia and have refocused the world's attention on the very area where the world's first civilizations emerged.

Electoral officials count votes in Afghanistan's first democratic presidential elections. Hamid Karzai won 55 per cent of the vote and was sworn in as President in December 2004.

2. ASIAN ENVIRONMENTS

ALMOST EVERY ECOSYSTEM ON EARTH CAN BE FOUND IN ASIA, A FEAT unmatched by any other continent. Some environments are virtually untouched by humans, such as the tundra of northern Russia. Others, such as some river valleys, fertile plains and forests, have suffered greatly under the pressures of Asia's enormous population.

FACT FILE

Mount Everest in the Nepalese Himalayas is the world's highest point at 8,850 m (29,035 ft). The first people known to reach its summit were Edmund Hillary and Tenzing Norgay in 1953.

TOP OF THE WORLD

The Himalayas are the world's highest mountains with 110 peaks over 7,300 m (23,950 ft). They straddle some 2,900 km (1,800 miles) along the border between India and Tibet (currently under Chinese control) and completely dominate the mountain kingdoms of Nepal and Bhutan. The Himalayas began forming around 40-50 million years ago when two tectonic plates met and began to crumple upwards against each other. This uplift continues today, and the relatively young Himalayas (in geological terms) are still growing by as much as 1 cm (0.4 inches) per year.

PLATEAU OF LIFE

The Himalayas form the southern edge of the Tibetan plateau – a vast area of mountains, gorges and deserts. This is the largest and highest plateau on Earth covering an area of around

The Tsho Rolpa glacier lake in the Himalayas on the border between Nepal and China.

14

2.5 million sq km (965,250 sq miles) and at an average elevation of over 5,000 m (16,400 ft). The plateau itself is sparsely populated. It is of great significance to the livelihoods of billions of Asians, however, because it is the source for several of the continent's major rivers, including the Yangtze, Ganges, Indus and Mekong rivers. The meltwater collected by these rivers are a lifeline for billions of people living downstream in the plains and river valleys of Asia. Besides providing water, these rivers carry enormous volumes of nutrient-rich sediment from the plateau. The Yangtze, for instance, is thought to carry and deposit up to 500 million tonnes (551 million tons) of sediment per year. Some of Asia's best farmland is found in the valleys and plains where this sediment is deposited. They include the Gangetic plains of India, and the Indus valley of Pakistan.

• • • • • • ▶ IN FOCUS: Fragile Earth

Much of Asia is affected by the continuing geological movements of the Earth's plates. On 26 December 2004 a major earthquake in the Indian Ocean provided tragic evidence of just how vulnerable Asia and its people can be to such events. The quake triggered a massive tsunami wave that travelled at speeds of up to 800 km (500 miles) per hour over thousands of kilometres, even reaching Africa. When it struck land the force of the water smashed into villages and coastal resorts in Indonesia, Thailand, India, Sri Lanka and numerous island chains, including the Maldives. An estimated 300,000 people were killed and millions left homeless. The United Nations believes it will take ten years for the area affected to recover.

The city of Banda Aceh on Sumatra, Indonesia was devastated by the December 2004 tsunami.

A man tills his smallholding on the banks of the Mekong River in Khon Chiam, Thailand.

RIVERS OF WOE

The vast amounts of water carried by Asia's rivers can sometimes turn them from life-givers into life-takers. The Huang Ho, or Yellow River, in China is particularly prone to flooding and has killed more people than any other river in the world. The Huang Ho has a very high silt content of up to 70 per cent by volume, and when swollen with abnormal amounts of water, the main river channel can not cope with the additional flow and bursts its banks. In 1931, the banks of the Huang Ho burst and caused the world's worst recorded flood. Over 4 million people were killed and more left homeless.

China's other major river, the Yangtze, is also prone to flooding and last experienced serious flooding in 1998. The Chinese government has taken measures to reduce the risk of future floods. In the upper Yangtze region millions of trees are being planted to absorb rainwater and reduce soil erosion, and in the floodplain, lakes are being restored that will allow floodwaters to disperse naturally rather than threaten settlements and farmland downstream.

INLAND SEAS

Western Asia is noted for its several inland seas. The Caspian Sea, shared by Azerbaijan, Russia, Kazakhstan, Turkmenistan and Iran is the largest inland water body in the world. It covers an area of 371,800 sq km (143,550 sq miles), which is roughly the same size as Japan or the US state of Montana. The Aral

•••••• ➤ IN FOCUS: The Aral Sea

The Aral Sea was once the fourth largest lake in the world with an area of 64,501 sq km (24,904 sq miles). In the 1960s the former Soviet Union diverted the waters of the Ama Dariya and the Syrdariya rivers, which feed the sea, into irrigation projects for growing cotton in what is now Uzbekistan. The flow of water into the Aral Sea was reduced dramatically and it had shrunk to less than half its size by 1995. Some former lakeshore communities found themselves living 100 km (62 miles) from the water. The Aral Sea is still shrinking today and is considered one of the world's worst ecological disasters.

Fishing boats lie abandoned on the former bed of the Aral Sea in Muynak, Uzbekistan.

Sea in Kazakhstan and Uzbekistan, and the Dead Sea in Israel and Jordan, are also inland seas. The Black Sea, which is shared by Turkey and five other countries, is almost an inland sea, but has a connection to the Mediterranean via the Bosporus Strait. This narrow channel is considered a geographical division between Europe and Asia.

WHERE THERE IS NO WATER

The largest desert in Asia is the Arabian Desert in southern Saudi Arabia. Also known as Rub' al Khali ('The Empty Quarter'), it covers an area of 2,330,000 sq km (899,614 sq

FACT FILE

Lake Baikal, near Russia's border with Mongolia, is the world's deepest lake at 1,637 m (5,371 ft). This incredible depth means the lake contains an estimated 20 per cent of the world's fresh surface water – the same as all five of North America's Great Lakes combined.

The sand dunes of the Arabian Desert near Riyadh in Saudi Arabia provide a popular tourist attraction.

FACT FILE

Asia has about 224,000 km of coastline, much of it intensively settled with fishing communities. Asia produces and consumes more fish and other marine products such as shellfish and seaweed, than any other continent.

miles) and is the largest continuous sand desert in the world. It is connected to another desert in northern Saudi Arabia called the Nafud, where giant sand dunes reach over 100 metres (328 feet) in height. Asia's other major deserts are the Gobi desert in Mongolia and China, the Takla Makan desert of north-western China and the Kara Kum desert in Turkmenistan – all among the world's ten largest deserts. These desert environments have very little water, and in the Arabian desert daytime temperatures can reach 54 degrees Celsius (129 degrees Fahrenheit). For this reason Asia's deserts are largely unpopulated, except around sources of water such as rivers, oases or where groundwater (stored beneath the surface) has been tapped.

DESERTIFICATION

Across Asia large areas are at risk of desertification, a process where soils are mismanaged (normally due to over-cultivation, over-grazing or deforestation) and take on desert-like characteristics, becoming unproductive and threatening livelihoods. The most severely affected countries include Pakistan, India, Iran, Mongolia and China. In 2004 desertification was thought to affect 27 per cent of China, which is home to around 400 million people. Its deserts were growing at an average rate of 2,460 sq km (950 sq miles) per year and the economic impact of declining agricultural yields was estimated at US$6.5 billion a year. Together with over 20 other Asian nations, China has formed a National Action Programme (NAP) to combat the threat of desertification. In China this has focused on planting trees in the areas most at risk of desertification. Up to 4 million hectares (9.884 million acres) of plantations are being created each year, and farmers are being paid to plant their land with trees instead of farming it.

FORESTS AND TUNDRA

Asian Russia is considered to be everything east of the Ural mountains. This area is frequently referred to as Siberia and accounts for around 75 per cent of Russia's total land area, but only 20 per cent of its population. Northern Siberia is made up mainly of arctic tundra, a bitterly cold environment with temperatures well below freezing for most of the year. The ground has a permanent layer of frozen soils (permafrost) that reaches depths of over 1,500 m (4,900 ft). To the south of the tundra is a habitat known as taiga. This is a marshy region of coniferous forests of fir, pine, larch, and cedar trees that covers around 60 per cent of Russia.

Sands from the Gobi Desert engulf Beijing in a storm during April 2000. The desert has expanded by 52,400 sq km (20,240 sq miles) from 1994 to 1999 and is now within 240 km (150 miles) of Beijing.

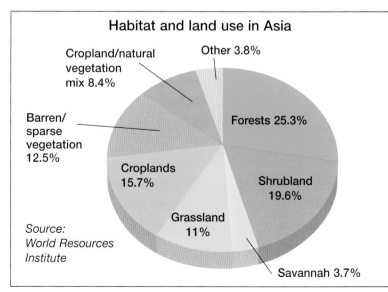

Habitat and land use in Asia

Other 3.8%
Cropland/natural vegetation mix 8.4%
Forests 25.3%
Barren/sparse vegetation 12.5%
Croplands 15.7%
Shrubland 19.6%
Grassland 11%
Savannah 3.7%

Source: World Resources Institute

It is the largest forest in the world – three times the size of the Amazon rainforest.

Forests are also a significant feature of South-east Asia. Indonesia, Malaysia, Thailand, Cambodia, Laos and Vietnam all have significant areas of tropical rainforest. Indonesia's rainforests are particularly important, as they are very species rich and make up around 10 per cent of the world's remaining rainforests.

Tundra dominates much of Siberia in eastern Russia, such as here in the Magadan region.

THE ASIAN MONSOON

Asia's climate varies from arctic conditions in the north to a tropical climate in the southeast. The range of climates is so complex that it is impossible to generalise, but an important climatic feature for much of Asia is the monsoon. The monsoon is a seasonal shift in wind patterns caused by the north-south movement of the sun and changes in the temperature of the Asian land mass. The summer monsoon occurs as the northerly movement of the sun heats the land mass, forcing hot air upwards and creating a pocket of low pressure. This condition draws in warm moist air from the Indian Ocean, heavily laden with rain. The monsoon and its rains are

Women weed rice paddies in the southern Indian state of Kerala. Like many Asian farmers, the success of their harvest is dependent on the rains of the Asian monsoon.

20

not entirely predictable, but normally reach Sri Lanka in early May and moves northwards to reach northern India by mid-July, with its arrival signalling the planting season for millions of farmers. In the northern winter monsoon, the cooling of northern and central Asia creates high pressure and reverses the air currents, driving cool dry winds southwards. This winter monsoon begins in northern India about September and reaches India's southern tip about mid November.

FACT FILE

Almost one quarter of the world's population depend on the Asian monsoon and its summer rains for their livelihoods.

The topography of Asia

Legend

▲ Mountain

0   500   1000 kilometres

0   500   1000 miles

ARCTIC OCEAN

East Siberian Sea

Laptev Sea

Bering Sea

PACIFIC OCEAN

S I B E R I A

CENTRAL SIBERIAN PLATEAU

Lena

Yenisey

Ob

Sea of Okhotsk

Sakhalin

Kamchatka

Kurile Islands

URAL MOUNTAINS

R U S S I A N S   F E D E R A T I O N

Ob

WEST SIBERIAN PLAIN

Lake Baikal

Hokkaido

KAZAKHSTAN

Aral Sea

Syr Darya

Lake Balkhash

MONGOLIA

GOBI DESERT

INNER MONGOLIA

NORTH KOREA

JAPAN

Honshu

TURKEY

GEORGIA

ARMENIA

Caspian Sea

AZERB.

UZBEKISTAN

Amu Darya

KYRGYZSTAN

TIEN SHAN

TAKLA MAKAN DESERT

SOUTH KOREA

Yellow Sea

Kyushu

LEBANON

SYRIA

ISRAEL

SYRIAN DESERT

JORDAN

IRAQ

Euphrates

Tigris

TURKMENISTAN

TAJIKISTAN

Yellow River

GREAT PLAIN OF CHINA

East China Sea

Ryukyu Islands

IRAN

IRANIAN PLATEAU

AFGHANISTAN

HINDU KUSH

C H I N A

Yangtze

KUWAIT

SAUDI

BAHRAIN

QATAR

The Gulf

PAKISTAN

Indus

PLATEAU OF TIBET

Salween

Brahmaputra

Xi Jang

Taiwan

PACIFIC OCEAN

ARABIAN DESERT

UAE

Gulf of Oman

THAR DESERT

HIMALAYAS

NEPAL

Ganges

Mt. Everest 5895m

BHUTAN

Mekong

Irrawaddy

Hainan Dao

Luzon

ARABIA

ARABIAN PENINSULA

OMAN

Arabian Sea

INDIA

BANGLADESH

MYANMAR

LAOS

South China Sea

PHILIPPINES

YEMEN

Gulf of Aden

Socotra

WESTERN GHATS

EASTERN GHATS

Bay of Bengal

Andaman Islands

THAILAND

CAMBODIA

VIETNAM

Gulf of Thailand

Mindanao

INDIAN OCEAN

SRI LANKA

Nicobar Islands

BRUNEI

Maldives

M A L A Y S I A

SINGAPORE

Borneo

Celebes

Moluccas

New Guinea

Sumatra

I N D O N E S I A

INDIAN OCEAN

Flores

Java

Timor

EAST TIMOR

Red Sea

21

3. THE PEOPLE OF ASIA

THE COMPOSITION AND WELLBEING OF ASIA'S POPULATION IS INCREDIBLY varied. It possesses the largest ethnic group in the world, the Han Chinese who number almost 1.2 billion people, but also has several of its smallest. The Jarawa of India's Andaman Islands are thought to number fewer than 300. In terms of wellbeing, the Japanese have the world's highest life expectancy of 81.5 years, compared with just 43 years in Afghanistan. Only 13 per cent of Afghanistan's population have access to safe drinking water, whilst in Japan it is universally available. Similar contrasts can be found throughout Asia's vast population, a population that accounts for almost 2 in 3 of the world's people.

A Pwo Karen woman carries clean water home from the village well near Omkoi in the Chiang Mai area of Northern Thailand.

FACT FILE

The Han Chinese are an ethnic group that make up around 92 per cent of China's population. They number more than the combined population of Europe and the United States.

GROWING NUMBERS

Asia's population grew rapidly during the second half of the last century from about 1.4 billion in 1950 to about 4 billion by 2005, an increase greater than the entire world population in 1950! Such rapid population growth is explained by dramatic improvements in medicine and in people's standards of living, leading to higher life expectancies and reduced infant mortality. In China, life expectancy at birth has increased from 36 years in 1960 to 71 years today, whilst in Iran infant mortality has fallen from 164 per thousand live births in 1960 to fewer than 34. As more children survive and adults live longer so the population begins to grow. In addition to these natural changes, large families are considered valuable in many parts of Asia for economic or cultural reasons. A large family means more available labour for working in the fields, the factory or around the home. Children also provide a form of social security where there is no government system as they will help to provide and care for their ageing parents. Some cultures also consider large families a sign of status, so parents may choose large families even when many children are unnecessary.

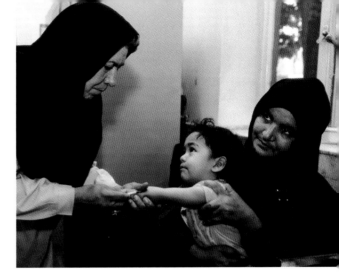

Asia has a youthful population with about 36 per cent of the population, or 1.4 billion people, below the age of 18. When Asia's young start their own families, the population will continue growing due to a process called population momentum. By 2050 Asia is expected to reach a population of around 5.2 billion. Only a handful of Asia's more developed nations, such as Japan, South Korea and the countries of the former Soviet Union, will see a decline in their population. This decline is due to lower birth rates and an ageing of the population in these countries.

A young girl being immunised in Tehran, Iran. Immunisation programmes have dramatically improved child survival rates in Iran and other Asian countries.

FACT FILE

At current growth rates, India will surpass China as the world's most populous nation in about 2045. By 2050, India will be home to over 1.5 billion people.

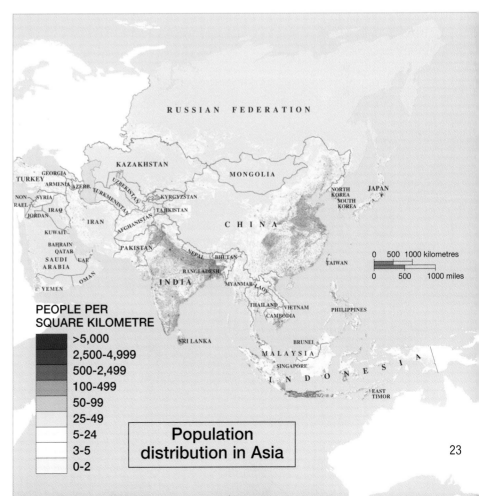

PEOPLE PER
SQUARE KILOMETRE

	>5,000
	2,500-4,999
	500-2,499
	100-499
	50-99
	25-49
	5-24
	3-5
	0-2

Population distribution in Asia

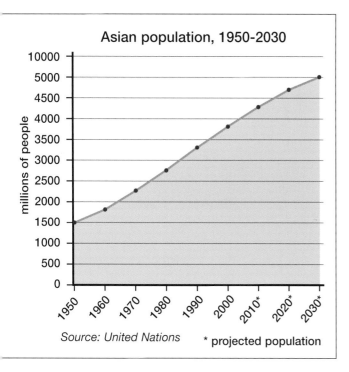

Asian population, 1950-2030

Source: United Nations   * projected population

FORCE OR CHOICE?

Rapid population growth places extreme pressure on governments to provide services such as health and education. India's population grew by over 170 million in the 1990s alone. In 1976, the Indian government of Indira Ghandi took drastic action to reduce population growth by introducing a policy of forced sterilization of the poor. It proved extremely unpopular and is widely blamed for the government's defeat in elections the following year. Several Indian states still offer financial incentives to people if they are sterilized, but they are no longer forced to do so.

Villagers in Orissa State, India watch a health education and family planning video from the back of a mobile health unit.

Today, most governments focus on helping parents make their own choices about the size of their families. This 'family planning' approach focuses on providing information and sometimes distributing free or subsidised contraceptives. When given such support, many parents voluntarily limit their family size. One difficulty in many Asian countries is that women do not enjoy the same rights as men and may not be given access to family planning services, particularly in countries dominated by strict Islamic beliefs where men dominate decision making. As a result, population growth in countries such as Yemen, Oman, Kuwait and Saudi Arabia remains very high at up to 3.6 per cent a year. This rate compares to an Asian average of 1.3 per cent and a world average of 1.2 per cent a year. Population experts agree that for population growth to slow across Asia, women must be given equal rights and empowered to make their own decisions about the number of children they have.

URBANISATION

After Africa, Asia is the world's least urbanised continent with 39 per cent of the population living in urban centres in 2003. In several countries, however, urbanisation is

FACT FILE

China's one-child policy is estimated to have prevented about 250 million births between 1980 and 2000. This is almost the same as the population of the USA!

●●●●●●● ▶ IN FOCUS: China's One Child Policy

In 1979, China introduced a policy limiting married couples to a single child. The only three exceptions made are for ethnic minority groups, when a first child is born with a disability, or when both parents are single children themselves. For other parents, a second child would result in a fine and could cost them their jobs or housing. In addition, the second child would be unregistered and so unable to attend school or receive healthcare. As a result of this policy many pregnancies are aborted, sometimes under great pressure from population officials. A cultural preference for boys – because they traditionally support ageing parents – has meant that more girls are aborted than boys. Some baby girls are even left to die so that parents may try again for a boy. These trends have resulted in an extremely unbalanced population. In 2000, figures suggested that 117 boys were born for every 100 girls and that this ratio could be as high as 131 to 100. A fierce debate continues about whether China's one child policy is a success story or a breach of basic human rights. The long-term impact for future population patterns are also unknown, but one likely outcome is that Chinese men who wish to marry will increasingly have to look for foreign brides due to a shortage of Chinese women.

A woman and her single child visit a local market.
China's single child policy is almost three decades old.

New high-rise apartment blocks spring up around the outskirts of Hong Kong - one of the most densely populated and heavily urbanised regions in the world.

substantially higher at 90-100 per cent in Singapore, Hong Kong, Israel, Qatar, Bahrain and Kuwait. In contrast, less than 20 per cent of the people in Cambodia, Bhutan and Nepal live in urban centres. In Asia's largest three populations, China, India and Indonesia, the urbanization rates are 39, 28 and 46 per cent respectively.

Despite relatively low rates of urbanisation, Asia is home to several of the world's largest cities. Tokyo, the most populous city in the world, had 35 million people in 2003. Any city with more than 10 million people is known as a mega-city and Asia had 11 of the world's 20 mega-cities in 2003. In addition to Tokyo they are Mumbai, Delhi and Kolkata in India, Shanghai and Beijing in China, Dhaka in Bangladesh, Jakarta in Indonesia, Osaka-Kobe in Japan, Karachi in Pakistan and Manila in the Philippines. Istanbul in Turkey is expected to join them soon as Asia's twelfth mega-city.

URBAN STANDARDS

Urban growth has been extremely rapid across much of Asia. Dhaka's population, for instance,

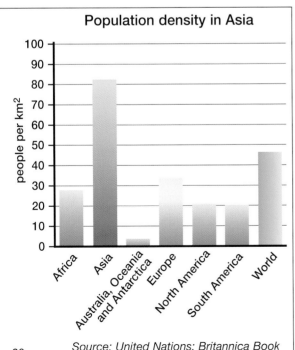

Population density in Asia

people per km^2

Africa · Asia · Australia, Oceania and Antarctica · Europe · North America · South America · World

Source: United Nations; Britannica Book of the Year 2004

FACT FILE

Asia has the highest population density in the world at almost 83 people per square kilometre (214 per square mile). Singapore and Hong Kong have almost 6,200 per sq km (16,000 per sq mile) whilst Macau has an incredible 16,530 people per sq km (43,010 per sq mile)!

An urban waterway clogged with refuse and sewage in Mumbai, India. Pollution like this is a serious health hazard to urban residents.

grew by over 6 per cent per year between 1975 and 2000, equivalent to adding 875 people every day. Few cities can keep pace with such growth and living conditions are often poor as a result. Jakarta, Indonesia, has a population of around 12.5 million people, but with no sewerage system. Around 73 per cent of Jakarta's households have septic tanks, but these pollute local water supplies and frequently overflow onto city streets. People without septic tanks simply defecate in the streets or in plastic bags that are then thrown into local ditches or rivers – known as 'wrap and throw' sanitation. With similar conditions in other Indonesian cities, illnesses such as gastroenteritis and typhoid are common. The cost of lost work time and treatment for these illnesses has been estimated at over US$4.7 billion a year.

FACT FILE

Asia includes 7 of the 10 most populous countries in the world – China, India, Indonesia, Pakistan, Russia, Bangladesh and Japan.

●●●●●▶IN FOCUS: The Orangi Pilot Project

Many Asian cities share Jakarta's problems, but some, such as the Orangi district of Karachi in Pakistan, have developed solutions. Home to around 1.2 million people, a self-help programme called the Orangi Pilot Project (OPP) was started in 1980 to improve sanitation. The community formed neighbourhood teams (according to the lanes (streets) within the settlement) and combined their labour and finances towards installing a basic sewage system. Each lane built and maintained its own system using locally supplied materials, and these were gradually connected to form a district system. Over 90,000 households are now connected to the system, which was built for just US$30 per household. The success of the OPP is now being copied in other Pakistani cities, as well as elsewhere in Asia.

HEALTHCARE

Countries such as Japan, South Korea, Singapore, Israel and much of the Middle East have healthcare comparable to that in Europe or northern America. Across the rest of Asia, the availability of healthcare varies considerably. In Kazakhstan, for example, there are about 260 people per doctor, whereas in Thailand this ratio increases to 3,333 people per doctor, and to over 16,660 in Bhutan and Nepal.

Across large parts of Asia, basic health needs such as clean water and sanitation are woefully short. In China, Indonesia and Vietnam, about one quarter of the

Healthcare facilities are stretched very thinly in countries like Nepal. This child is being examined by western-trained nurses at Pokhara in Nepal. There is a shortage of trained medical staff in Nepal and many other Asian countries.

population lacks access to safe water. In Oman, Laos and Cambodia this number increases to over 60 per cent of the population. Shortages of these basic needs are significant because the majority of diseases in Asia (typhoid, diarrhoea, hepatitis A and cholera) are related to poor quality water and sanitation.

MAJOR DISEASES

Malaria is a disease carried by mosquitoes and is found across large parts of Asia, from Afghanistan through Pakistan, India and into South-east Asia as far as south Indonesia. Southern China and Yemen in the Arab peninsula are also affected. Although preventable and treatable with anti-malarial drugs, malaria parasites are now resistant to drugs in many countries. In addition, the drugs are too expensive for many poorer communities.

HIV infection rates are increasing rapidly in Asia and many experts believe it could soon replace Africa as the centre of the global HIV epidemic. There are already up to 11 million people

living with HIV/AIDS across
Asia, and over a million new
people were infected in 2003
alone. South-east Asia is the
region with the highest infection
levels, while the fewest are in the
Middle East and East Asia.
Poorer communities are most
affected because they are
generally less educated and less
aware of the ways in which HIV
is transmitted.

A counsellor delivers an HIV
education seminar to community
members in a district of Jakarta,
the Indonesian capital. HIV/AIDS is
relatively new to Indonesia but is
spreading quickly.

AN EDUCATED CONTINENT

Education is highly valued across
Asia and has helped the continent
to develop a highly skilled and able workforce. Companies
and governments in other parts of the world, such as Europe,
Australia, or North America, actively recruit Asian graduates
to fill skills gaps within their own labour force. This practice
is especially true in the medical, engineering and computer
industries. Not all Asians benefit from an education, however.
Less than three-quarters of children in southern Asia attend
primary school, and a third of these will fail to complete their
basic education (five primary years). Poverty is normally the
cause for these drop outs, but in agricultural societies parents
may choose to keep children from school in order to help in
the fields or around the home. In Muslim communities, girls
may be denied the opportunity to go to school at all. Under
the Taliban regime (1995 - 2001) in Afghanistan, girls were
banned from school, and those being educated in secrecy
risked severe punishment. Even in the more moderate Muslim
societies of the Middle East, girls frequently have less
opportunity than boys to complete their schooling.

4. ASIAN CULTURE AND RELIGION

DAILY LIFE IN ASIA IS STRONGLY INFLUENCED BY PEOPLE'S RELIGIOUS beliefs: festivals and religious events are celebrated by millions in some of the biggest gatherings of humanity on the planet. Islam, Christianity, Hinduism, Judaism, Buddhism and Sikhism are major global religions that all have their origins in Asia. In Eastern Asia more localised belief systems, including Shinto from Japan, and Confucianism and Taoism from China, are found.

PRIMARY RELIGION

Most Asian countries are dominated by a single religion. Saudi Arabia, Iran, Iraq, Pakistan, Afghanistan, Turkey and Azerbaijan are all over 90 per cent Islamic. Buddhism is the majority religion in Cambodia, Thailand, Bhutan, Burma and Laos whereas Hinduism dominates in India and Nepal. Christianity dominates in the Philippines and Judaism in Israel. China is unusual because it is officially an atheist state – having no sanctioned religion. Buddhism and Christianity are both practised in China, however, and the government has become more tolerant of these in recent years. In fact, China is said to have one of the world's fastest growing Christian populations.

The dragon dance, here being performed in the Chinese capital Beijing, is a traditional part of the Chinese New Year celebrations. The spread of Chinese culture means Chinese New Year is now celebrated in many western nations too.

RELIGION AND CONFLICT

The majority of Asians live peacefully alongside each other irrelevant of their differing beliefs. In some parts of the continent, however, people with different belief systems clash over issues such as political control or over competing rights to disputed territory. Kashmir has been an area of dispute since 1947 when India became independent from Britain and was partitioned into India (mainly Hindu) and Pakistan (mainly Islamic). Kashmir lies right on the border of this divide. It is part of the northern Indian state of Jammu and Kashmir - the only Indian state to have a mainly Islamic population. Pakistan has long claimed that, because of this, Jammu and Kashmir should be part of Muslim Pakistan. India, however claims sovereignty over Jammu and Kashmir after it was ceded to India in October 1947. Thousands have died in the ongoing conflict over the state.

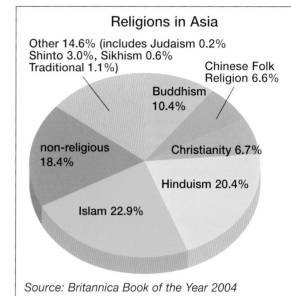

Religions in Asia

Other 14.6% (includes Judaism 0.2% Shinto 3.0%, Sikhism 0.6% Traditional 1.1%)

Chinese Folk Religion 6.6%

Buddhism 10.4%

Christianity 6.7%

non-religious 18.4%

Hinduism 20.4%

Islam 22.9%

Source: Britannica Book of the Year 2004

SACRED CITY

The city of Jerusalem in Israel is a spiritual centre for three world religions – Christianity, Islam and Judaism. Every year millions of people travel to the city to visit its numerous religious sites. These sacred places include the Western 'Wailing' Wall (the holiest Jewish site), the Church of the Holy Sepulchre (Christianity's holiest site where Jesus is said to have been crucified) and the Dome of the Rock (from where it is believed Muhammad, the founder of Islam, ascended to Heaven). With its shared religious claims, Jerusalem is one of the most contested pieces of land in the world and lies at the heart of tensions within the Middle East.

The Dome of the Rock in Jerusalem, Israel, is the oldest surviving structure in the Islamic world dating back to AD 691. It is built on Haram esh-Sharif (Temple Mount) which is sacred to both Muslims and Jews.

PILGRIMS AND FESTIVALS

Asia is witness to some of the world's greatest pilgrimages and several of the largest festivals ever known. One of the greatest spectacles on earth is the annual Hajj that takes place in Mecca, Saudi Arabia. It is the ultimate pilgrimage for all Muslims and one that every Muslim will try to make at least once in his or her life. Up to 2 million people gather in Mecca each year to perform a series of rituals that together comprise the Hajj.

FAMILY VALUES

The family is an important institution in Asia. Families gather for festivals such as the Hindu celebration Diwali or the Chinese New Year. Marriages are also important events and in India can attract thousands of guests from enormous extended families. Families are also an important form of economic support. Children have

IN FOCUS: Maha Kumbh Mela

Hindus celebrate many different festivals, but nothing compares to the Maha Kumbh Mela (Great Pitcher Festival). It takes place every three years and rotates between four locations in India. The Maha Kumbh Mela at Allahabad, where the Ganges, Yamuna and mythical Saraswati rivers meet, is considered the most sacred location. In 2001, over 110 million pilgrims came to bathe in the waters and perform a ritual washing away of their sins.

Pilgrims and sadhus (holy men) gather for the 2001 Maha Kumbh Mela at Allahabad.

traditionally cared for their elders, and wealthy relatives are expected to assist those who are less fortunate. These close family ties extend into the business world and many of Asia's most successful companies are built around a single family. The 'chaebols' of South Korea are a good example of these ties. Chaebols are large groups of companies that are normally controlled by a single family. The biggest chaebols have become world-known brands and include Hyundai, Samsung, LG and Daewoo.

A GLOBAL INFLUENCE

Some aspects of Asian culture have a global influence, for example the popularity of its cuisine, with Chinese, Thai, Indian and Japanese dishes today being served up worldwide. Martial arts such as tae kwon do (Korea), kung fu (China) and judo and karate (Japan) have emerged from Asia to become major world sports. Asian philosophies have also spread widely, including feng-shui from China and Japan and yoga from India. Artistically, Asian designs and colour patterns are used around the world, influencing architecture, clothing, furniture and interior design, and even gardening.

The Hyundai shipyard in Ulsan, South Korea is the largest in the world. It is owned by Hyundai, a family run company known as a chaebol.

Yoshihiro Akiyama (blue) throws Nyamkhuu Damdinsuren of Mongolia to win a contest during the September 2003 World Judo Championships held in Osaka, Japan.

FACT FILE

Indian food is the most popular dish for eating out (including takeaways) in the UK. London has more Indian restaurants than Mumbai, Kolkata, Dehli and Madras combined!

33

A craftsman carves a wooden Garuda sculpture in Bali, Indonesia – well known for its woodwork.

Elaborate costumes and make up add to the drama of Kathakali dancing in southern India.

SKILLED ARTISANS

Asia's artisans are remarkably skilled and produce a wide range of goods. Indonesia is well known for woodcarving and batik, China for pottery and painting, India for hand-printed textiles and jewellery, and Iran for its Persian carpets and rugs. Several art forms are uniquely Asian including a form of writing, calligraphy, originating in China and paper folding, origami, originating from Japan. Japan has also made popular the Chinese art of growing miniature trees, known as 'bonsai'.

PERFORMING ARTS

India's movie industry is arguably the most famous of Asia's performing arts today, and India produces more films than any other country. The industry is centred in Mumbai (formerly Bombay) and has become known as 'Bollywood'. Nearly all the films include music and dancing and are normally based around a love story and a main hero or heroine. The movies' elaborate sets and beautiful costumes are a link to more traditional performing arts in India. One of these is kathakali dancing from Kerala in southern India. Kathakali dancers are famous for their colourful three-dimensional make up and costumes. The dancers tell traditional stories by performing a combination of dance and mime. The movement of their eyes, the whites of which are dyed red for the performance, plays a particular role in expressing the emotions of the stories.

SPORT IN ASIA

Sport is popular across most of Asia and a wide variety of sports are played. Some are sports played around the world, such as soccer, cricket and basketball, but others are unique to Asia such as sumo wrestling in Japan or camel racing in the Middle East. Asia has produced many of the world's leading athletes in sports as varied as gymnastics, badminton, archery and weightlifting.

South Korea's Im Dong-hyun aims during the men's archery competition at the Athens 2004 Olympic Games. He went on to help win the men's team event for South Korea.

At the 2004 Olympic Games in Athens, Greece, South Korea confirmed itself as the world's leading archery nation. Sung Hyun Park won the gold medal in the women's archery and, together with her teammates, also took the team event. South Korea also took gold in the men's team archery. Badminton was completely dominated by Asian nations with South Korea winning the men's doubles, Indonesia's Taufik Hidayat winning men's singles and China claiming the women's and mixed medals.

Watching sport in Asia is almost as important as participating in them, with sporting events attracting huge audiences. When the Indian cricket team is playing, city streets grind to a halt as everyone follows the fortunes of the team. South Koreans are similarly committed to their national football team, and national celebrations occurred when the team reached the semi-finals of the 2002 World Cup which South Korea jointly hosted with Japan. In 2008 the attention of the sports world will be fixed on Beijing when China becomes the third Asian nation, after Japan (1964) and South Korea (1988), to host the Olympic Games.

35

5. NATURAL RESOURCES IN ASIA

ASIA IS RICH IN NATURAL RESOURCES AND PLAYS A PARTICULARLY KEY role in global energy supplies. For this reason, it has become a region of intense international attention. Critics in the USA, the UK, and abroad have accused both the United States and Britain of intervening in the Middle East region, not for peace and stability as they claim, but to gain access to the region's oil wealth.

OIL WEALTH

Oil derricks and rigs fill the landscape around the Caspian Sea in Azerbaijan, a country rich in oil. The oil is extracted from both offshore and onshore operations.

At the end of 2003 Asia (including the Russian Federation) accounted for 75 per cent of the world's proven oil reserves and about 52 per cent of its production. This immense oil wealth is overwhelmingly focused in the countries of the Middle East with Saudi Arabia, Iran, Iraq, Kuwait and United Arab Emirates (UAE) having the most significant reserves. Among other Asian nations the oil reserves of the Caspian Sea region are thought to be the most significant. To date these have been underutilised because of political disputes over who owns the reserves and practical difficulties of how to export the oil from the region. Azerbaijan and Kazakhstan are leading the growth in the oil industry around the Caspian Sea however, and have increased their oil production by 70 per cent since 1992. New pipelines have been built connecting the oilfields of the Caspian Sea to oil terminals on the Black Sea

and Mediterranean Sea. From here oil is then transported by tanker to key oil markets in North America, Europe and Eastern Asia, particularly Japan.

NATURAL GAS

Asia also accounts for substantial gas reserves with 78 per cent of proven reserves and 47 per cent of global production at the end of 2003. The Russian Federation is the region's main source of natural gas with 27 per cent of world reserves and 22 per cent of global production. Other significant sources include Iran, Qatar, Saudi Arabia and UAE, but they are also found in Bangladesh, Myanmar, Malaysia and Vietnam amongst others. Bangladesh's gas reserves are its only significant source of energy and are therefore of vital importance to its economy. Some controversy exists over the potential export of Bangladeshi gas to neighbours such as India as Bangladeshis believe it should be used to benefit Bangladesh directly and not sold to earn foreign exchange. Plans include using natural gas as fuel for motor vehicles and for generating electricity. It can also be used to make agricultural fertilisers that are in high demand in Bangladesh.

Pipelines carry natural gas from the gas fields to the refinery in the Yamburg area of Russia. Natural gas is a key Russian export to meet European energy needs.

COAL

Asia has around 41 per cent of the world's known coal reserves with the majority of these located in The Russian Federation, China and India. Over half of the world's coal (51 per cent) is produced in Asian countries, with China alone accounting for

33.5 per cent of global output. Much of China's coal is used to fuel its rapidly expanding industrial economy, but this dependence on coal has had serious environmental implications because China's coal is mainly 'brown coal', which is particularly high in sulphur and releases large quantities of sulphur dioxide as it is burned. When sulphur dioxide is mixed with water vapour in the atmosphere, it forms acid rain, which damages plants and buildings and contaminates water sources when it falls to earth. Large volumes of carbon dioxide, one of the main gases associated with global warming, are also released. China produces about 12 per cent of the world's carbon emissions, second only to the United States' total of 24 per cent.

HEP

Asia's rivers provide several countries with a resource that can be used to generate electricity. Known as hydro-electric power (HEP), this process works by channelling water through turbines that generate electricity as the force of falling water causes them to turn. Bhutan, Nepal, Laos, Kyrgyzstan and

An open pit coal mine creates a giant scar on the landscape at Manzhouli, in Inner Mongolia, China. China's rapid industrialisation of recent years has been heavily reliant on its coal reserves for energy.

Tajikistan depend on HEP for over 90 per cent of their electricity supplies. Other Asian nations with significant HEP dependency include North Korea, Vietnam, Afghanistan, Japan, India and China. China and India have both pursued large-scale dam building projects in recent years to harness their rivers for HEP. Several of these projects have caused controversy because of their potential social and environmental impacts. The Three Gorges HEP project on China's Yangtze river, for example, will displace about 2 million people and submerge an estimated 1,650 settlements when it is completed in 2009. Environmental experts are also concerned that pollutants released during the flooding of industrial facilities could seriously contaminate the river.

Tarbela HEP Dam on the Indus River in Pakistan rises 148 meters high and is 2743 meters in length. Completed in 1977, the embankment contains 126,151,570 cubic meters of earth and rock, the largest volume ever used in a structure of its kind.

MINERALS

Asian nations produce a wide range of the world's key non-fuel minerals including iron ore, bauxite, tin, chromium, titanium, fluorspar and copper. Several countries have a lead role in the global supply of minerals. China produced about 54 per cent of the world's fluorspar – a raw material for making plastics and optical products – in 2002 and 21 per cent of its iron ore,

Wood is transported home by a young boy in Pakistan. The use of wood for cooking and heating in many Asian countries is placing the region's forests under increasing pressure.

FACT FILE

Between 1990 and 2000 Indonesia's forests were shrinking at a rate of about 1,312,000 hectares (3,242,000 acres) each year. Wildlife, such as the already endangered orangutan, is severely threatened by such forest clearance.

which is used to make steel. Kazakhstan accounted for 18 per cent of the world's chromium (used to strengthen steel) and Indonesia for 9 per cent of its copper.

FORESTS

Much of Asia's original forest cover has been cleared to make way for agricultural land or for settlements. Forest area has also declined due to the use of forests for fuelwood, construction materials or general timber. Wood is still important as an energy source, mainly for cooking, in several Asian countries, including India and China. In India fuelwood was used by around 21 per cent of urban households and 62 per cent of rural households to meet their cooking needs in 2000.

The tropical forests of South-east Asia are renowned for their high quality tropical timbers. In 2002, Malaysia was the world's biggest exporter of tropical logs and Malaysia and Indonesia were the leading exporters of tropical sawnwood and tropical plywood. The main markets for tropical timber from South-east Asia are Japan, China, the United States and Europe. In addition to logging in areas approved by Asian governments, there is a considerable volume of illegal logging in South-east Asia. Indonesia is especially affected and some experts believe that the illegal logging of Indonesia's forests equals, and maybe even exceeds, legal logging. The Indonesian government is trying to stop illegal logging through export bans (introduced in 2001) and increased policing of forests, but these measures have had minimal impact to date.

FISHERIES

Asia is the world's leading producer of fish, with China alone accounting for about 18 per cent of the world catch. Japan, Indonesia, the Russian Federation, India, Thailand and the Philippines are also key fishing nations, but fishing is important across much of the continent. It provides the main source of protein in the diets of millions of Asians and is also a major employer with about 30 million fisherfolk employed across the continent. Asia's fisheries are considered a vital resource for meeting the food needs of its growing population, but there is concern that if it is not carefully managed, fishing waters could become depleted.

FACT FILE

China, Japan, Indonesia, the Russian Federation, India, Thailand and the Philippines accounted for about 41 per cent of the global fish catch in 2000.

●●●●▶ **IN FOCUS:**
Aquaculture

China is at the forefront of a revolution in fishing known as aquaculture. This is where fish are farmed in ponds to produce food for human and/or animal consumption. Between 1970 and 2000, the contribution of aquaculture to total global fish production increased from 3.9 per cent to 27.3 per cent. Asia accounts for about 90 per cent of current world aquaculture production and is also the area of fastest growth. One unique form of aquaculture practised in China and Cambodia is the practice of raising fish alongside rice, the region's staple crop. This practice is done by raising fish in the flooded paddy fields and has proven to be a highly productive farming system as the fish also help to fertilise the rice.

The Jugalchi fish market in Busan, South Korea is one of the largest in Asia. Fisheries are an important element of the Asian economy.

6. THE ASIAN ECONOMY

ASIA IS SECOND ONLY TO AFRICA AS THE POOREST REGION OF THE world and includes several of its poorest countries, such as Bangladesh, Cambodia, Nepal, Tajikistan, Nepal and Laos. In Japan, however, Asia also has the world's second largest economy (after the United States). Several of the world's wealthiest nations, including Hong Kong, Singapore and Kuwait are also in Asia.

A woman works in a cornfield in northern Pakistan.

A MIXED ECONOMY

Traditionally agricultural, Asia's economic structure changed dramatically during the second half of the twentieth century, and Asia is today a truly mixed economy. Its industries include many of the world's leading manufacturers, and it is also home to an increasing proportion of the world's service industries. In 2000, the economic contributions by sector for the continent as a whole were about 8 per cent for agriculture, 35 per cent for industry and 57 per cent for services. These averages, however, hide the continued importance of agriculture in several Asian economies. In Iran, for instance, agriculture still made up about 21 per cent of the total economy in 2000 whilst in China, Pakistan and India the figure was about 18, 24 and 28 per cent respectively. Agriculture is also important to Israel and Turkey, both of which have developed high value agricultural exports in fruits and vegetables to the nearby European markets.

INDUSTRIAL GROWTH

Asia's industrial growth came about following the World War II and was led by Japan. Japan focused on high-tech industrial production in its post-war rebuilding. Relatively poor in its own natural resources, Japan's industries looked to its Asian neighbours for the supply of raw materials and converted them into finished products for export to the more developed economies of Europe and North America. By the 1970s Japan had become a major world economy and one of the leading producers of cars, steel, ships, electrical products and other manufactured items.

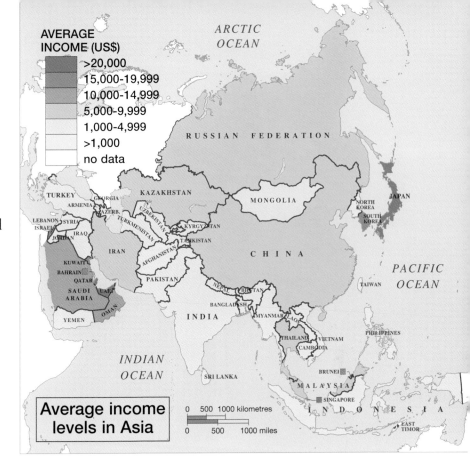

Average income levels in Asia

Japan's success has been built around a business system called 'Soga-Shosha' that develops enormous corporate conglomerates in which a family of individual businesses combine their resources. In such a system, trade takes place as much within the conglomerate as it does with external customers and suppliers. A Japanese company might, for example, buy the rights to mine iron ore in Indonesia and sell the ore to its steel plant in Japan. The steel may then be sold to Japanese automobile factories in Europe to make cars that are sold on to Japanese car retailers in the USA. By controlling the chain of production and trade Japanese businesses have amassed great wealth. South Korea is one of several Asian, and indeed world, countries to adopt

Japan and South Korea have built a reputation for producing high quality electronic goods such as computers, mobile phones and cameras.

elements of the Soga-Shosha business system. Known as 'chaebols' in South Korea, such systems have been equally influential in the growth of South Korea's economy.

TIGERS IN CRISIS

Between the 1960s and mid 1990s, four Asian economies – Taiwan, Singapore, Hong Kong and South Korea – achieved incredible economic growth by focusing on export industries and protecting their domestic markets from imported foreign goods. They became known as the 'Asian Tigers' and were soon joined by Thailand, Malaysia, Indonesia and the Philippines. These economies depended on foreign markets for their success but, in the mid 1990s, changes in global currency markets began to make their goods more expensive. Exports fell dramatically and imports increased as exchange rates made imported goods cheaper.

The Petronas Towers in Kuala Lumpur, Malaysia were the tallest buildings in the world until overtaken in 2004 by the Taipei 101 building in Taiwan. The Petronas Towers were completed just as the Asian economic crisis struck and remain half empty as the economy can not support full occupancy.

In 1997 Thailand was forced to devalue its currency in an effort to make its products more affordable. The global financial markets reacted badly and withdrew funds from South-east Asia throwing the whole region into decline. Billions of dollars were lost from the value of the economies.

ASIA'S RECOVERY

After millions of job losses and numerous company closures, the Asian tigers are today on their way to pre-crisis levels of growth and prosperity. The recovery in Asia is being led by China and India. They managed to escape the Asian crisis and have now shown over a decade of consistent growth. The Indian economy expanded by an average of 5.7 per cent a year between 1992 and 2002 and China's economy grew even faster at about 10 per cent annually. This progress compares with annual growth in the USA and UK of just 3.2 and 2.5 per cent respectively.

China's growth has focused on manufacturing industries. The service industry is also expanding rapidly and China hopes to make Shanghai the financial centre of Asia, replacing Tokyo and Hong Kong. Central to China's success has been its opening up to capitalist markets and allowing overseas companies to invest in China. China's engagement with the free market economy was most clearly indicated in 2001 when China joined the World Trade Organisation (WTO) – the main global regulator of world trade.

Like China, India's growth has been due to a mix of both industry and services. It has developed particular strengths in the Information Technology (IT) industry and is now a major centre for the global computer and software industry. Technological developments, such as the Internet and low cost international phone calls, have also allowed India to become a world leader in the service sector. India is able to offer high quality services for a much lower cost than in Europe, North America or even eastern Asia. Several UK bank and insurance companies have transferred their call centres to India due to cost savings of about 40 per cent. This process is known as 'offshoring' and has seen thousands of jobs move from countries like the United States and UK to India.

The Pudong district of Shanghai in China was mainly agricultural land until 1990, but is today at the heart of Shanghai's transformation into the financial capital of Asia.

A woman answers calls in Bangalore, India at one of the city's many call centres. This one handles calls relating to Texan insurance regulations and parts specifications for a Detroit car maker in the USA.

Tourism boom?

The economy of the Middle East is dominated by oil, but tourism is a fast growing sector too. Israel has long attracted tourists who come to visit the Holy Land, but other key attractions include the historic sites of Jordan and Turkey, which also benefits from coastal tourism along Turkey's beautiful Mediterranean beaches. Dubai has one of the fastest growing tourist sectors developed around shopping, water sports, desert adventures and luxury hotel breaks. Between 1990 and 2003 the number of tourists visiting the Middle East increased from 10 to 28 million visitors per year and for 2001-2002 (a difficult time for the tourist industry in the wake of terrorist attacks on the USA), tourism in the Middle East grew by 17 per cent – faster than in any other region of the world.

Informal economy

Although Asian service sectors are expanding, many service jobs remain part of a vast informal economy, an unregulated cash-based economy in which people normally pay little or no tax on their incomes. Typical services include portering, street vendors, rubbish collection, laundry services and low-skilled manufacturing jobs. Recent studies have estimated

The Mahalakshmi municipal dohbi ghats in Mumbai, India are a scene of frantic activity. Hundreds of dhobis (washermen and women) wash and dry thousands of articles of clothing every day as part of India's enormous informal economy. Services such as this are often performed by workers in the informal economy.

that the informal sector accounts for 67 to 78 per cent of non-agricultural employment in Bangladesh, Pakistan, Thailand, Indonesia and the Philippines. Women make up a disproportionate number in the informal sector as they are often prepared to work for less. The textile industry in Asia is renowned for its use of low-paid female workers in the informal economic sector.

FACT FILE

Uzbekistan is the world's only double landlocked country - it and all of its immediate neighbours are landlocked.

●●●●●●▶ IN FOCUS: Rebuilding the Silk Road?

The original Silk Road is one of the oldest known trading routes in the world (since Roman times) and connected eastern China with markets in Europe, Africa and the Middle East via a network of long distance paths that crossed the Asian continent. Since 1996, there have been plans to rebuild the Silk Road as a trade route for the future. The idea originated in the former Soviet nations that now form a group commonly referred to as Central Asia (including Uzbekistan, Turkmenistan and Azerbaijan). Since becoming independent of the Soviet Union, the economies of these regions have struggled to develop, not least because they are extremely isolated from their potential markets in Europe and eastern Asia. In addition, they inherited infrastructure (roads, rail networks, bridges and so on) that was in a poor state of repair. A new Silk Road would bring economic benefits to Central Asia, opening up trade with the rest of the continent and with Europe to the west. It would also strengthen regional trade within Central Asia. The United Nations, Asian Development Bank, European Union and the US government have all expressed support for the idea, because it would provide an export route for Central Asia's valuable energy resources.

A rugged section of the Karakoram Highway as it crosses from Pakistan into China. The Karakoram Highway is part of the famous Silk Road trade route that crosses the Asian continent.

47

7. Asia in the World

Asia is geographically located between the two existing world power centres of North America and Europe. This key position not only facilitates commerce and trade, but also allows for the spread of ideas and cultural values. In the closing decades of the twentieth century, however, Asia has established itself as much more than a conveniently located continent. It is fast emerging as a major world power in itself with strong and vibrant economies and a pivotal role in global politics. China and Russia, for example, have long been two of the five permanent members of the UN Security Council - the global body for ensuring peace and security in the world. Russia, along with Japan, is also a G8 country – a group of the world's eight most industrialised countries.

China and Russia hold permanent seats on the UN Security Council, meeting here at its headquarters in New York.

Power from Within

One of the most fundamental ways in which Asian countries influence the world is in the supply of crude oil – the basis of virtually all modern and energy hungry economies. This influence is wielded through an organisation called OPEC – the Organization of Petroleum Exporting Countries - that was formed in 1960. Its membership comprises three African states (Libya, Algeria and Nigeria), Venezuela in South America, and seven Asian countries (Saudi Arabia, Iran, Iraq, Kuwait, Indonesia, Qatar and United Arab Emirates). Between them, they control about 80 per cent of the world's oil reserves and about 40 per cent of world oil production.

By having its members agree on production quotas, OPEC is able to alter the amount of oil entering the world markets and thereby influence the global oil price. This control was demonstrated most dramatically in 1973 when OPEC policies raised oil prices first by 70 per cent and then again by a further 130 per cent. Many countries faced major fuel shortages whilst others accrued large debts as they struggled to buy fuel at the higher prices. So severe were the effects of the OPEC price increases that they have been blamed as a cause of the debt crises currently facing many of the world's poorer nations.

Some economists question whether OPEC is as powerful today as in the past, because of the increase in oil supplied by non-OPEC members, including the USA, Mexico, UK, Norway and the Russian Federation. What is clear, however, is that OPEC demonstrated the significance of oil and, more specifically, of Asian oil to world affairs. This importance continues today and is often said to be at the heart of international interests in creating peace and stability in the Middle East and Central Asia. Lasting peace in the region would secure oil supplies and prices and in doing so bring greater stability to the global economy. In contrast, continued instability can cause fluctuating oil prices that have an impact on economies far removed from the region itself.

An intricate network of pipes forms part of the massive Ras-Tanura oil refinery in Saudi Arabia. Saudi Arabia is a key member of OPEC, an organisation able to influence the supply and price of the world's oil.

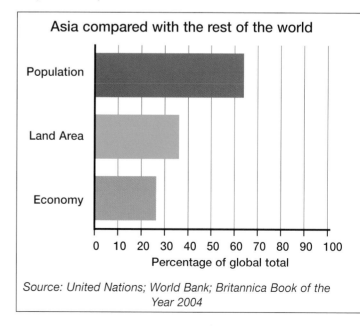

Asia compared with the rest of the world

Source: United Nations; World Bank; Britannica Book of the Year 2004

GLOBAL HOTSPOTS

At the start of the twenty-first century, Asia has more hotspots than anywhere else in the world. These are places where conflict, tension or instability threatens the lives of the people living there and, in some instances, those of a much wider area. Key hotspots include North Korea, Israel/Palestinian territories, Afghanistan, Iraq and Kashmir in northern India. Afghanistan and Iraq, for example, are struggling to rebuild after years of dictatorial rule by the Taliban in Afghanistan and Saddam Hussein in Iraq. These regimes behaved in a totalitarian and ruthless manner, often ignoring the human rights of not only their own citizens, but also those of neighbouring states. Following terrorist attacks in the United States on September 11th, 2001, links were made between the terrorists and the Taliban regime in Afghanistan. A coalition led by the United States took military action to remove the Taliban as part of a global 'war on terror,' and the Taliban fell from power in December 2001.

The United States later led a campaign to remove Saddam Hussein from power in Iraq. His regime had used chemical weapons in the past and there were concerns that such weapons of mass destruction (WMD) could fall into the hands of terrorists in the future, and hence it was believed that Iraq posed an immediate threat to U.S. security. The US-led attack on Iraq brought about the collapse of Saddam Hussein's regime in April 2003. Although such weapons of mass destruction were not found once the US and its allies entered Iraq, both Iraq and

An Iraqi man throws stones at a statue of President Saddam Hussein as it falls in central Baghdad April 9, 2003. U.S. forces assisted Iraqi civilians in toppling the statue to symbolise the end of Saddam's regime. Democratic elections were held in Iraq in January 2005 to elect a new interim government.

Afghanistan are now heading towards democratic self-governance. Tensions between rival groups, however, continue to boil over. International troops remain based in Afghanistan and Iraq in an effort to maintain peace and security.

IN FOCUS: Israel, the Territories and the Palestinians

Israel and Israeli-controlled territory that formerly made up the land called Palestine occupy a narrow slice of Asian land between the Mediterranean Sea and the Jordan River. For over half a century, this land has been one of the most contested territories in the world, in large part because both Israel (which was founded in 1948 as a Jewish state) and Palestinians consider it to be their rightful homeland. A series of armed conflicts between Israel and its Arab neighbours in 1948, 1967 and 1973 saw Israel gain even greater control over the disputed territories. These gains included complete control over Jerusalem and important Muslim landmarks. An estimated 3.7 million Palestinians have been displaced as a result of these tensions and currently live in neighbouring Arab states and in the Israeli-controlled West Bank and Gaza Strip. Attempts to broker peace between Israel and the Palestinians have been led by the United States, but disagreements over control of Jerusalem and the return of Palestinian refugees have hampered progress. Talks have been further hampered by Jewish settlements in the West Bank and Gaza, Palestinian suicide bombings against Israeli targets, and Israeli military action in Palestinian areas. A new ceasefire and round of diplomatic talks between Israeli and Palestinian leaders in January 2005 has raised hopes for peace in the region.

Palestinian youths throw stones at Israeli soldiers during clashes in the centre of the West Bank City of Ramallah.

North Korea is a country of particular concern to the international community as it is known to possess nuclear weapons that could be used against other states. North Korea is one of the most isolated countries in the world and one of only a few remaining communist states. It has maintained a fragile ceasefire with South Korea since a war divided Korea into two in 1950-53. Governments around the world are concerned that North Korea could use its weapons if the conflict were to resume. The international community is putting great pressure on North Korea to enter into talks to find a lasting peace for the Korean Peninsula. The US government, along with China, Japan, Russia and South Korea, are playing a key role in these negotiations.

The Great Wall of China is one of the major attractions drawing tourists to China, soon to become the world's number one tourist destination.

WORLD DESTINATION

Asian influences in the areas of cuisine, cinema, design, philosophy and religion among others, have spread throughout the world and become part of daily life for people living well beyond the borders of the continent. The people of Asia themselves have also spread far and wide as evidenced by the number of Asian communities that have been established overseas. Cities including London, New York, Paris, and Sydney today have their own Chinatowns. Communities of immigrants from Bangladesh, India, Pakistan, Vietnam, Thailand and many others are also found in a wide range of countries.

One result of this spread of Asian culture has been to increase the desire of people to visit Asia themselves. Low cost air fares and

A tourist approaches a group of Indian elephants at the Pinnawela Elephant Orphanage in Kegalle, Sri Lanka. Asia's wildlife is a key asset for its tourist industry.

improved communications have made it easier to find out about and visit even quite remote locations. High profile events such as the World Cup, held in South Korea and Japan in 2002, have also boosted the appeal of Asia. In 2002 there were about 145 million tourist arrivals in Asia, more than double the 62 million of 1990. The top destinations were China (36.8 million), Hong Kong (16.6 million), Malaysia (13.3 million) and Thailand (10.9 million). China has a particularly thriving tourist industry and, in 2002, was ranked fifth in the world for both arrivals and earnings (income from tourism). China is also becoming a significant generator of tourism as incomes rise and its population enjoys greater travel opportunities. This is significant for other Asian nations as travel within regions accounts for about 80 per cent of all tourism. A further boost to China's tourist industry is expected when its capital, Beijing, hosts the Olympic Games in 2008.

FACT FILE

By 2020, China is expected to become the world's leading tourist destination and the fourth largest generator of tourists.

8. ASIAN WILDLIFE

THE WILDLIFE OF ASIA IS EXTREMELY DIVERSE AND INCLUDES many unique species such as the blind freshwater river dolphins of the Ganges, Yangtze, Indus and Mekong rivers. These animals are today extremely endangered as a result of human interference or destruction of their natural habitat. The same is true for much of Asia's other wildlife, including the Asian elephant, the Bengal and Siberian tiger, the Sumatran rhinoceros and the Giant Panda in China.

A young giant panda plays on a tree in the Sichuan Province of China. Most of the 1,596 wild giant pandas recorded in 2004 live in Sichuan Province. Their numbers have increased by 40 per cent between 2000 and 2004 due to improved habitat conservation.

DECLINING HABITATS

The orangutan is a good example of the dangers facing Asian wildlife. Orangutans (meaning 'people of the forest' in Malay) are found in Indonesia and Malaysia, but deforestation for timber or for agricultural land and settlements has severely reduced their natural habitat. In 1900 there were about 318,000 orangutans in the wild but, today, there are thought to be fewer than 20,000 left. Conservation experts believe they may be disappearing at a rate of up to 2,000 per year. Orangutans face particular problems because their breeding cycle is very slow. Females do not begin to mate until around 15 years of age and will wait around 8 years between offspring – the longest parental care period of any primate except for humans. These delays mean the population reproduces itself very slowly. Indonesia has taken steps to try and protect orangutans by creating national parks, such as Tanjung Putting formed in 1982. Policing the national parks has proven difficult, however, and illegal logging remains widespread. Tanjung Putting alone is estimated to lose about US$ 8 million worth of timber every year.

PEOPLE AND WILDLIFE

A consequence of declining Asian habitats is that people and wildlife are increasingly brought into contact and conflicts can arise. In 2002, a herd of around 100 Asian elephants crossed into northern Bangladesh from Meghalaya state in India. The elephants migrated across the border when the forests they were living in were cleared to make way for a new highway. Crossing into Bangladesh the elephants caused enormous damage to forests, homes and crops and killed 13 people with many more injured. By late 2004 Bangladesh was threatening to kill the rampaging elephants unless they were returned to India. Although Bangladesh agreed elephants should be protected, they also stated that they could not be allowed to terrorise, injure and kill local people. Between 1997 and mid-2004 some 180 people are known to have died in clashes with elephants across Bangladesh.

A young orangutan with its mother in Sumatra, Indonesia. Orangutans are threatened by human activities and economic development.

FACT FILE

Indonesia is one of the most species-rich countries in the world. It contains about 10 per cent of the world's tropical rainforest, 17 per cent of its bird species, 16 per cent of reptile and amphibian species and 12 per cent of mammal species.

•••••• ▶ IN FOCUS: Project Tiger

One of Asia's most successful conservation examples is 'Project Tiger' in India. In 1900 there were an estimated 40,000 tigers in India, but a 1972 census recorded only 1,827 tigers – a decline of over 95 per cent. Project Tiger was launched in 1973 to establish protected reserves in India's remaining tiger habitats and enforce the conservation of the species. Human activity was banned completely from the core of each reserve, but a buffer zone around each has enabled local people to continue using the environment for their own needs, such as gathering of fuelwood. Nine reserves were initially established in 1973-74 and contained 268 tigers, but the numbers have steadily increased to reach 27 reserves by 2003 and a protected population of 1,576 tigers. Project Tiger has attracted worldwide praise for its conservation work, and its reserves have become a major tourist attraction with visitors paying large sums to see the biggest of the world's cats. India launched 'Project Elephant' in 1991-92 to try and repeat the success of Project Tiger.

A mass of tourists watch India's greatest predator, the tiger, in Bandhavgarh National Park, one of the parks involved in Project Tiger.

WORKING WITH WILDLIFE

Many of Asia's wild animals have been domesticated for human benefit. Elephants have long been used to move logs in the timber industry and also form the centrepiece of many colourful festivals in India. Elephants are also increasingly being used to provide tourist rides or shows. The use of elephants for this purpose, however, has been questioned. In 2000 a British tourist was killed in Thailand when a bull elephant performing a tourist show gouged her with his tusks. In desert regions, camels are used for transporting goods as they are ideally suited to the harsh desert environment. In India's desert city of Jaipur, camels are a regular feature of the bustling city traffic. Buffalo or cattle are used by many Asian farmers to help plough the land, though this is declining as tractors become more widespread. A more unusual use of wildlife is found on the Yangtze river in China where fishermen use tamed cormorants to catch fish. These expert birds dive for fish from the edge of the boat and are prevented from swallowing the catch by a ring around their necks.

Owners give their camels a drink at the Pushkar Camel Fair in Rajasthan, northern India. The annual camel fair is the world's biggest and draws thousands of traders and their valued animals. Camels are still used for transporting goods in Rajasthan.

FACT FILE

In May 2004 a new flightless bird species, named the Calayan rail (*Gallirallus calayanensis*), was discovered in the forests of Calayan, an island of the Philippines.

9. THE FUTURE OF ASIA

At the start of the twenty-first century Asia is a continent on the brink of realising its full potential. Its economies are growing well, its people are healthier and better educated than ever before, and it is playing an ever more important role in world affairs. Led by the emerging powers of China and India and under the existing influence of Japan and the 'tiger economies', Asia can look ahead with great optimism to the future.

South Korean border guards patrol the demilitarised zone (DMZ) that has separated South and North Korea since 1953 and remains the last Cold War frontier in Asia.

REGIONAL STRENGTH

One of Asia's greatest benefits is its regional strength. Between them Asian nations control a significant percentage of the world's resources, and they also share the biggest potential market for finished products. As incomes rise, it is expected that Asia will increasingly look to trade within the region and become less dependent on its historical markets in Europe and North America. If plans such as the rebuilding of the Great Silk Road are realised then intra-regional trading will be further strengthened.

STABILITY AND PEACE

Of vital importance to the future of Asia is an end to the conflicts and tensions that have plagued some parts of the continent for over half a century. There remains, for example, a tense relationship between North and South Korea, heightened in 2005 by the revelation that North Korea possessed nuclear weapons. The

Israeli/Palestinian conflict also remains unresolved despite US and international pressure to steer the two parties along a roadmap for peace. In addition, there is a need to help rebuild the lives of those affected by years of instability and conflict in Afghanistan and Iraq following the overthrow of their brutal regimes in 2001 and 2003, respectively. For a people so used to violence and internal conflict, becoming a stable and peaceful society is a continuing struggle. The international community is concerned that a failure to bring about peace in these troubled parts of Asia could spawn more terrorist groups such as Al Qaeda.

SUSTAINABLE DEVELOPMENT

Meeting the needs of its massive population without further degrading its natural environments will be a key challenge for Asia's future. This is the challenge of sustainable development. Issues such as habitat destruction, overuse of resources and pollution are already serious concerns for large parts of the continent. The fear is that as incomes and living standards rise and approach those of North America or Western Europe, these issues will become ever more serious. The number of cars in China, for instance, has more than doubled from just 5.8 million in 1990 to over 13 million by 2002, bringing associated problems of pollution with it. One thing is clear and that is the continent that witnessed the dawn of the world's first civilisations will play a major role in determining the direction and sustainability of those in the future.

China's booming economy has led to new problems such as road congestion and pollution, here in Beijing. Overcoming such problems is vital to the sustainable development of the country.

STATISTICAL COMPENDIUM

Sources: UN Agencies, World Bank and Britannica

Nation	Area (sq km)	Population (2003)	Urbanization (% population) 2003	Life expectancy at birth 2002 (in years)	GDP per capita (US$) 2002	Percentage of population under 15 years 2003	Percentage of population over 65 years 2003
Afghanistan	652,225	23,897,000	23.3	43.0	N/a	44	3
Armenia	29,743	3,061,000	64.4	72.3	3,120	20	10
Azerbaijan	86,600	8,370,000	50.0	72.1	3,210	27	7
Bahrain	694	724,000	90.0	73.9	17,170	27	3
Bangladesh	147,570	146,736,000	24.2	61.1	1,700	35	3
Bhutan	47,000	2,257,000	8.5	63.0	1,969	42	4
Brunei	5,765	358,000	76.2	76.2	19,210	30	3
Cambodia	181,916	14,144,000	18.6	57.4	2,060	39	3
China	9,572,900	1,304,196,000	38.6	70.9	4,580	24	7
Georgia	69,492	5,126,000	51.9	73.5	2,260	18	14
Hong Kong	1,092	7,049,000	100.0	79.9	26,910	16	12
India	3,165,596	1,065,462,000	28.3	63.7	2,670	32	5
Indonesia	1,937,179	219,883,000	45.6	66.6	3,230	29	5
Iran	1,645,258	68,920,000	66.7	70.1	6,690	29	5
Iraq	435,052	25,175,000	67.2	63.0	N/a	39	3
Israel	20,320	6,433,000	91.6	79.1	19,530	27	10
Japan	377,819	127,654,000	65.4	81.5	26,940	14	19
Jordan	89,326	5,473,000	79.0	70.9	4,220	37	3
Kazakstan	2,724,900	15,433,000	55.8	66.2	5,870	25	8
Korea, North	122,762	22,664,000	61.1	63.0	N/a	26	7
Korea, South	99,268	47,700,000	80.3	75.4	16,950	21	8
Kuwait	17,818	2,521,000	96.3	76.5	16,240	25	2
Kyrgyzstan	199,900	5,138,000	33.9	68.4	1,620	32	6
Laos	236,800	5,657,000	20.7	54.3	1,720	42	3
Lebanon	10,400	3,653,000	87.5	73.5	4,360	30	6
Macau	21	464,000	98.9	79.0	N/a	21	7
Malaysia	329,733	24,425,000	63.9	73.0	9,120	33	4
Maldives	115	318,000	28.8	67.2	4,798	39	4
Mongolia	1,564,116	2,594,000	56.7	63.7	1,710	32	4
Myanmar	676,577	49,485,000	29.4	57.2	1,027	32	4
Nepal	147,181	25,164,000	15.0	59.6	1,370	40	4
Occupied Palestinian Territory	6,263	3,557,000	71.1	72.3	N/a	45	3
Oman	309,500	2,851,000	77.6	72.3	13,340	41	3
Pakistan	796,095	153,578,000	34.1	60.8	1,940	40	3
Philippines	300,076	79,999,000	61.0	69.8	4,170	36	4
Qatar	11,437	610,000	92.0	72.0	19,844	24	3
Russia	17,075,400	143,246,000	73.3	66.7	8,230	16	13

Saudi Arabia	2,248,000	24,217,000	87.7	72.1	12,650	40	3
Singapore	646	4,253,000	100.0	78.0	24,040	21	8
Sri Lanka	65,610	19,065,000	21.0	72.5	3,570	25	7
Syria	185,180	17,800,000	50.1	71.7	3,620	38	3
Tajikistan	143,100	6,245,000	24.7	68.6	980	36	5
Thailand	513,115	62,833,000	31.9	69.1	7,010	23	7
Timor-Leste	N/a	778,000	7.6	49.3	N/a	40	N/a
Turkey	779,452	71,325,000	66.3	70.4	6,390	28	6
Turkmenistan	488,100	4,867,000	45.3	66.9	4,300	34	4
United Arab Emirates	83,600	2,995,000	85.1	74.6	22,420	19	2
Uzbekistan	447,400	26,093,000	36.6	69.5	1,670	34	5
Vietnam	331,041	81,377,000	25.7	69.0	2,300	30	5
Yemen	555,000	20,010,000	25.6	59.8	870	45	3

GLOSSARY

Chaebol A group of companies in South Korea that operate in different fields but are all part of one parent company. The largest chaebols have evolved from family run businesses.

Cold War Used to describe differing political and economic ideals between capitalist democracies (led by the USA) and socialist communists (led by the former USSR) that dominated world politics between 1945 and 1990.

Deforestation The removal of trees, shrubs and forest vegetation.

Groundwater A body of water that is found beneath the earth's surface. Groundwater is often extracted for human use using boreholes and wells.

HIV/AIDS Human Immunodeficiency Virus (HIV) is a deadly virus spread by unprotected sex or contaminated needles or blood supplies. It can develop into Acquired Immuno-Defiency Syndrome (AIDS), which is fatal. Expensive drugs can keep people alive, but there is no cure.

Homo sapiens sapiens The scientific name of modern human beings.

Hydro-electric power (HEP) A type of energy generated by fast-flowing water flowing through turbines.

Independence When a country wins the right to control its own affairs.

Infant mortality The number of babies, out of every 1,000 born, who die before the age of one.

Infrastructure Networks that allow communication and/or help people and the economy to function. Examples include roads, railways, electricity and phone lines.

Islamic Of or relating to the faith of Islam, such as Islamic buildings or designs.

Maritime Relating to the ocean or sea or to shipping and sailing. Also to describe being close to the sea such as a maritime nation being next to the ocean.

Origami The art of paper folding that originates from Japan.

Partition The process by which the Indian sub-continent was divided into modern day India, Pakistan and Bangladesh following independence from Britain in 1948.

Population momentum The process by which a population continues to grow in absolute numbers even when the rate of growth has slowed. The continued growth is normally due to a large proportion of the population yet to enter child bearing age.

Service sector The part of the economy that provides services such as banking and retail.

Urbanization The process of a region or country becoming urbanized, meaning that its population increasingly lives in urban areas (towns or cities).

FURTHER INFORMATION

BOOKS TO READ:

A River Journey: The Ganges by Rob Bowden (Hodder Wayland, 2003)

A River Journey: The Yangtze by Rob Bowden (Hodder Wayland, 2003)

Changing Face of China by Stephen Keeler (Hodder Wayland, 2003)

Changing Face of India by David Cumming (Hodder Wayland, 2005)

Changing Face of Japan by Lewis Lansford and Chris Schwarz (Hodder Wayland, 2004)

Changing Face of Malaysia by Aiden Glendinning and Jim Holmes (Hodder Wayland, 2004)

Changing Face of Thailand by Terry Clayton (Hodder Wayland, 2005)

Countries of the World: Japan by Robert Case (Evans Brothers, 2002)

Countries of the World: China by Carol Goddard (Evans Brothers, 2004)

Rivers Through Time: Settlements of the Indus River by Rob Bowden (Harcourt Education, 2005)

USEFUL WEBSITES:

http://www.survival-international.org
Survival International is a worldwide organization supporting tribal peoples.

http://news.bbc.co.uk/1/hi/world/asia-pacific/default.stm
BBC News Asia-Pacific page with latest news and country profiles. Also has a link to Middle East and South Asia pages.

http://edition.cnn.com/ASIA/
CNN home page for Asia news and information.

INDEX

ABOUT THE AUTHOR

Rob Bowden is a freelance author and photographer specialising in geographical and environmental issues and with a particular interest in less developed regions. He has made several trips to research and photograph books in Asia including, most recently, India and South Korea. He has also lectured in geography and development studies at Sussex, Brighton and Keele universities in the UK.